"The "Quote?"

Jarmel Bell, MSE

AuthorHouse™
1663 Liberty Drive
Bloomington, IN 47403
www.authorhouse.com
Phone: 1-800-839-8640

First published by AuthorHouse 1/27/2011

ISBN: 978-1-4567-2702-4 (sc)
ISBN: 978-1-4567-2703-1 (e)

Library of Congress Control Number: 2011900642

Printed in the United States of America

Any people depicted in stock imagery provided by Thinkstock are models, and such images are being used for illustrative purposes only. Certain stock imagery © Thinkstock.

This book is printed on acid-free paper.

Dedication

To my best men (Jeremy Bell, Terance Crockett, Terrell Goff, Sean Richardson, Carlton Young), you guys have been there for me anytime that I have needed you. You guys have always been there to listen to me, give me advice, and put me back in my place if I was out of line. lol. I love you guys. Thanks for everything.

Acknowledgements

I would first like to give an honor to God, who is the head of my live. Through God's mercy and grace, I have been truly blessed.

I would like to thank my wonderful wife (Sheneka Rashelle Bell) for having my hand in marriage and assisting me with the development of the "Quote." I Love You

I would like to thank all 3 of my daughters (Skyla , Shira , Eden) for being such great children. They are the best. I Love Y'all

I would like to thank my parents (John & Terrie Bell) for always supporting me. I Love You

I would thank to thank my sister and brother (Jacqueline Michelle, Jeremy Nathaniel) for keeping me in check. I have the best brother and sister. I Love Y'all

I would like to give a special thank you to Cantrell McGee for the helping me develop this book into the great leadership guide that it has become. Thank You

I would like to thank all the people that gave me valuable input with the concept of the book.

∞ Preface ∞

The words of the wise, famous, or simply experienced, can have a profound impact upon the behaviors and attitudes of others. Often, we underestimate the impressions made by carefully chosen words; words that have the power to embolden, encourage, uplift, and motivate one to greatness. With these concepts in mind, I have undertaken the task of composing this book with the intent to inspire young people to make better choices in their daily interactions with others. This will help build strong, permanent character traits that will help guide them to success and happiness.

The Quote is a fascinating compilation of lessons, each focusing on a particular area of human behavior. The format is in *Phases,* each with its own set of *Blocks* that provide insight into why certain behaviors are desirable or undesirable, and how they can be improved upon. *The Quote* is not a mere collection of "self-help" strategies, but is aimed at assisting young ones, those for whom it is possible to redirect their attitudes, to meet the challenges of growing up to be caring, productive and contributing members of society.

Throughout this written work are direct quotes of learned individuals, whose opinions and philosophies have spanned generations, yet have lost none of their intrinsic value as words to live by. The purpose behind using quotes is two-fold: 1.) To supplement the lesson being taught, and 2.) to inspire the reader to pay close attention to the words of others; in effect, to be an effective listener. I might also stress that, the quality of some one else's words is not determined by whether they are famous or not. Wisdom can be harvested from the most humble of individuals, as well as the most celebrated. It is not confined to those known for the greatest intellect, but it is found within a vast array of socio-economic circles – among the great and the small. What matters most is whether one's words are meaningful and if they can be of beneficial to others.

Each phase of *The Quote* addresses character issues and is laced with the appropriate quotes that help substantiate the reasoning contained therein. The famous quotes used in this book were carefully chosen to highlight the main points of the lessons. They are meant to engage the reader in the thought process of the writer being quoted and to then relate the writer's words to his or her own life experiences. Hopefully, the reader can then ascertain the true meaning behind the words of the author.

It is my personal goal to ensure that each reader of *The Quote* is guaranteed to take away from these pages at least one gem of knowledge, if not several, which can be put to practical use in his or her life. This will spark genuine self-esteem, integrity, and a sense of well-being that will contribute to lifelong success.

I am writing this book to talk about my experiences and positive results from my interactions with students who display behavioral, emotional, and self-esteem issues. When you consider the entirety of their issues, you end with a person's character. When you take into account a person behavior, habits (good or bad), their emotional state, their self-esteem (confidence), these characteristics comprise that individual's character, which he is.

I have researched and studied these behaviors for the last 12 years; collecting data from the study of selected subjects. The primary conclusion that I have reached is that no two people behave the same, under the same set of circumstances. Further, I have concluded that, although people can make the same mistake or misbehave exactly in the same manner, their reasons for these actions may be completely different, and in many cases, the person is clueless regarding why he made the ill-advised choice.

"The Quote" was written to teach people how to make smart choices through character education. People have consistently made poor and uneducated decisions throughout life because of a lack of critical thinking skills. Thinking is the key ingredient to being considered a "Smart" person.

Research has shown that people who tend to exhibit poor behavior predominantly have difficulty predicting consequences prior to their actions. When a person has the tools necessary to make smart choices, he/she has put themselves in a position to have a positive outcome. As an educator, I want to see every person achieve success.

During the past few years, I have developed a curriculum that will assist students in finding themselves and equipping them with the tools they need to become successful. One person's tool box may be totally different from that of another. For this reason we must be responsible for our own actions, thereby assuming responsibility for our own success.

The program that I have developed has three phases comprised of nine blocks. Each phase has a different focus point. Phase I- Self-Respect, Phase 2-Respect of Others, and Phase 3 – Leadership. Three blocks are assigned to each phase. The nine blocks consist of Respect, Integrity, Responsibility, Compassion, Citizenship, Tolerance, Commitment, Resilience and Accomplishment. While reading this book, you will discover how the nine blocks are equally distributed throughout the three Phases. The beauty of working with people who do not have their "Smart Tool Box" yet is that you must be patient but consistent with them. The average time frame that is required to complete each Phase is one school year. The program understands the uniqueness of every person and provides every person who reads this book to become successful.

The layout of this book is structured so that a person can make steady progress through The Quote program. The program also allows for individuality and requires each participant to take ownership of their own success.

Table of Contents

Phase 1- Self Respect

Block I Respect

Block II Integrity

Block III Responsibility

Phase 2- Respect of Others

Block IV Compassion

Block V Citizenship

Block VI Tolerance

Phase 3- Leadership

Block VII Commitment

Block VIII Resilience

Block IX Accomplishment

SELF-RESPECT

-proper esteem or regard for the dignity of one's character

"Men are respectable only as they respect"
Ralph Waldo Emerson

What does it mean to respect yourself? People spend the majority of their time caught up in what's going on in the lives of others, being nosy, gossiping, being disrespectful, and directing their focus everywhere but on themselves. It is time for the individual to invest in himself!

Individuals who show respect for themselves are typically inclined to show sincere regard for the work and property of others. Self-respect goes hand in hand with the idea of self-value; appreciating the positive aspects of your own personality and the unique attributes that you alone possess.

A person who respects himself is generous with compliments toward others. He or she shows consideration for the freedom, privacy, and dignity of other individuals and treats others as he appreciates being treated. Courtesy is a key component in cultivating self-respect because when one is courteous, he builds within himself a deeper sense of self-worth. He or she becomes the kind of person worthy of emulating. Tolerance for the differences in others and patience in dealing with the inadequacies of others contribute to the degree to which one can respect himself.

Liking who we are, caring for how others view us and striving to develop the type of personality that draws others to us can be a challenge. We can be motivated by the good examples set by those we admire. For instance, think of someone you consider to be outstanding, exemplary in conduct and well-liked. Reflect on traits this individual possesses that make him or her special. Then, imagine how you can cultivate such traits, but in your own unique way. Talk with someone you admire and ask them about their life experiences, goals and how they attained them, and how they view him/her.

Courage is a fine attribute. Don't be afraid to stand up for what is right, even at the risk of being unpopular. Stand out as different and be proud to do so. Do what you believe is best and this will increase your self-worth.

Rather than being harshly critical of yourself, focus on the many good qualities that make you who you are. Never compare yourself or your achievements to those of others. Know that you are deserving of respect from others, but most of all from yourself!

"They cannot take away our self-respect if we do not give it them"
Mahatma Ghandi

Self-Respect   Facilitator Guide

Introduction: Define respect.
                    Why is respect important?
                    Give an example of a respectful person.

Examples of qualities that directly relate to a person that shows respect (create a list)

- Courtesy
- Sensitive
- Self-Respect
- The way to treat people. (do unto others the way you want them to do unto you)

Are you a respectful person? Why or why not?

Group session questions:

- What do you (as a person) stand for?
- What are your values?
- How do you take care of yourself?
- How is your appearance?
- How do you take care of your body?
- Do you have bad habits or good habits?
- How do people address you? How do you address other people?

Write two paragraphs on the importance of you being a respectful person.

Peer Worksheet

Self-Respect

Name: _____

Date: _____

Define respect. _____
_____

Why is respect important? _____
_____

Give an example of a person that is respected. _____
_____

List 5 things that are instilled in a respectful person:

    1. _____

    2. _____

    3. _____

    4. _____

    5. _____

Notes:

_____
_____
_____

What is the importance of being a respectful person?

_____
_____
_____
_____
_____
_____
_____
_____
_____
_____
_____

MANNERS

-a person's outward bearing; way of speaking to and
treating others, this includes proper etiquette

"A man's own good breeding is the best security against other people's ill manners"
Lord Chesterfield

A good indicator of solid character in a person is that of good manners. Manners are a reflection of one's upbringing and provide insight into the type of environment in which you grow up. Good manners include showing consideration for the feelings of others, without having to be prompted to do so.

Some classic examples of showing good manners include: saying a greeting when someone comes into the room; responding when being greeted; and addressing one's elders with respect. Manners are an intricate part of a sterling character. People remember when they have been accorded courtesy and this will influence how you are perceived by other members of society. Good manners are not pretentious. You don't "put on airs", pretending to be someone you are not, kindness and consideration for civility should originate from within, motivated by a desire to "shine" as a genuinely caring individual.

"Better were it to be unborn than to be ill bred."
Sir Walter Raleigh

Unlike fads that come and go, good manners never go out of style. They are timeless, priceless, and wear well into the golden years. Many young people fear using good manners because of what others may think of them. Never hesitate to display fine manners! Even if you initially are reluctant to appear different from your peers, it is well worth the effort to cultivate proper etiquette and make good manners a part of your character. Practice keeping elbows off the table, not talking with your mouth full, waiting politely before speaking when others are talking, saying "Please and Thank you," and not insisting on being first in line. As you model these behaviors, it is likely that your friends will begin to emulate you. If they choose not to follow your example, you can still be content with the knowledge that you are being true to yourself and these habits will contribute to future happiness, achievements and success!

"Consideration for others is the basis of a good life, a good society"
Confucius

Manners   Facilitator Guide

Introduction: Define manners.

  Why are manners important?

  Give an example of a person having manners.

Example of qualities that directly relate to a person with manners (create a list)

- Saying "Yes ma'am," No ma'am,"" Yes sir,"" No sir"
- Opening doors for women
- Saying Courtesy
- Addressing adults properly when they call on you (not saying uh, what, etc…)
- Helping people that are having difficulties

Are you a person with proper manners? Why or why not?

Group session questions:

- Why should a person have manners?
- How can you tell if a person has manners?
- How do you practice having proper manners?
- Name a person that doesn't have good manners?
- How do people respect people without manners?

Write two paragraphs on the importance having/showing proper manners.

Manners

Name: _____

Date: _____

Define manners. _____

_____

Why are manners important? _____

_____

Give example of a person that has manners. _____

_____

List 5 things that are instilled in a person with proper manners:

    1. _____
    2. _____
    3. _____
    4. _____
    5. _____

Notes:

_____

_____

_____

What is the importance of a person having manners?

_____

_____

_____

_____

_____

_____

_____

_____

_____

_____

_____

HYGIENE

-a condition or practice conducive to the preservation of health, as cleanliness

"Bathe twice a day to be really clean, once a day to be passably
clean, once a week to be avoid being a public menace"
Anthony Burgess

Good hygiene is critical to being safe, healthy and a general part of your well-being. Some practices always to remember include a daily bath or shower, and if you have especially dry or sensitive skin, it may be best to use a mild soap but do not neglect regular bathing. Also remember to brush and floss your teeth. Good dental care can help prevent disease and infections in other parts of the body. Use soap when washing hands after using the restroom, before meals, and anytime they are dirty. Remember, using deodorant or antiperspirant and keeping your hair shampooed regularly contribute to your keeping your body fresh. Nails should be kept clean and well-groomed. Pay attention to your ears, as well.

Another reason for why good hygiene is so important is that it helps you take care of yourself physically as well as emotionally. People often have infections because they don't take good care of themselves physically, which can lead to emotional difficulties. To avoid physical problems associated with poor hygiene, consider how others are affected when you don't exercise good hygiene habits. Perhaps, you have been around someone who does not smell pleasant, or who does not always wear clean clothes. Imagine what others think of such a person. Often the impression you give by your appearance and how clean and fresh you present yourself is the first and only opportunity you will have to state who you are and what your values are.

"Hygiene is two thirds of health"
Lebanese Proverb

Everyone should strive to keep a neat and clean appearance. It is not necessary to have a closet full of designer clothing, but you should always be dressed in something neat and clean. Clothing should be properly washed, ironed and kept on hangers to avoid wrinkles. Even if you have a very limited wardrobe, you can do your absolute best to maintain it until you can afford to do better. Never feel pressured to compete with your peers when it comes to designer labels and expensive clothing. It is necessary that you preserve the cleanliness of your attire, while keeping your personal hygiene at the top of the list of good habits.

"Man does not live on soap alone; and hygiene, or even health, is not much good unless
you can take a healthy view of it – or, better still, feel a healthy indifference to it."
Gilbert K. Chesterton

Hygiene

Introduction: Define hygiene
Why is hygiene important?
Give an example of a person having good hygiene.

Some examples of qualities that directly relate to a person with good hygiene (create a list)

- Taking baths daily
- Use deodorant daily
- Brushing teeth regularly
- Combing your hair
- Looking good, smelling good, having a swagger about you, no matter how big or small you are

Are you a person with good hygiene? Why or why not?

Group session questions:

- Why should a person have good hygiene?
- How can you tell if a person has good hygiene?
- How do you practice having good hygiene?
- Name a person that doesn't have good hygiene?
- How do people respect people without good hygiene?

Write two paragraphs on the importance having good hygiene.

Peer Worksheet

Hygiene

Name: _____
Date: _____

Define good hygiene. _____
_____

Why good hygiene is important? _____
_____

Give some examples of people that have good hygiene's. _____
_____

List 5 things that are instilled in a person with good hygiene:

    1. _____
    2. _____
    3. _____
    4. _____
    5. _____

Notes:

_____
_____
_____

What is the importance of a person having good hygiene?

_____
_____
_____
_____
_____
_____
_____
_____
_____
_____
_____

APPRECIATING YOURSELF

-involves being grateful or thankful for your initiative in a number of different ways

"Every day is my best day. This is my life; I am not going to have this moment again."
Bernie Siegel

Expressing appreciation for one's own good qualities go hand-in-hand with emotional health and well-being. Becoming aware of the positive aspects of your own personality may not come easily, and is often confused with "blowing your own trumpet." Even if you are shy, easily embarrassed, and find it difficult to accept compliments or praise, it is essential that you develop self appreciation.

At times we may not feel good about ourselves and might tend to seek approval from others. Rather than looking to someone else to fulfill the need for acceptance, it is best to recognize the many good things about ourselves! To begin the necessary steps in appreciating yourself, learn to take good care of yourself. It sounds simple, but is not necessarily an easy thing to do. It requires being consistent and disciplined in your effort. For instance, are you eating properly and receiving enough rest? Do you regularly exercise and engage in healthful recreation? How do you view entertainment? Do you value and listen to good music and read interesting books that increase your knowledge and awareness of the world around you? These are necessary habits to cultivate and help form a deep and lasting appreciation of who you are.

"It is of practical value to learn to like yourself. Since you must spend so much time with yourself, you might as well get some satisfaction out of the relationship."
Norman Peale

Self-acceptance is similar to self-appreciation. Your perception of yourself will reflect how you act and behave. Be positive. Think good thoughts about the experiences in which you have been successful. Avoid comparing yourself to others. Everyone has his and her own talents, abilities, strengths and weaknesses. No two people are entirely alike; not even identical twins. Develop the talents that you possess and be generous in sharing them with others. As you do so, your skills will increase, giving you more reasons to be proud, confident and genuinely appreciative of the person you are becoming.

"By appreciation, we make excellence in others our own property."
Sophocles

Appreciating Yourself   Facilitator Guide

Introduction: Define appreciating yourself
              Why is appreciating yourself important?
              Give an example of a person appreciating them self.

Qualities that directly relate to a person appreciating themselves (create a list)

- Believing in themselves
- Doing things for himself (does it offend or hurt others?)
- Keeping yourself up (hygiene, self-respect, practicing good manners)
- Taking pride in your values

Are you a person that appreciates them self? Why or why not?

Group session questions:

- Why should a person appreciate himself?
- How can you tell if a person appreciates himself?
- How do you practice appreciating himself?
- Name a person that appreciates them self. How can you tell?
- How do people respect people that don't appreciate himself?

Write two paragraphs on the importance of appreciating yourself.

Peer Worksheet

Appreciating Yourself

Name: _____

Date: _____

Define appreciating yourself. _____

_____

Why is appreciating yourself important?_____

_____

Give an example of a person that appreciates them self. _____

_____

List 5 things that are instilled in a person that appreciates them self:

    1. _____

    2. _____

    3. _____

    4. _____

    5. _____

Notes:

_____

_____

_____

What is the importance of a person having self appreciation?

_____

_____

_____

_____

_____

_____

_____

_____

_____

_____

_____

TRUSTWORTHINESS

*—the concept of consistency of actions, values, methods;
measures principles, expectations, and outcomes*

"Integrity has no need of rules."
Albert Camus

Building character through integrity requires a willingness to accept oneself for who you truly are. Understand that character and integrity are integral parts of emotional self-esteem. Integrity means steadfast adherence to a strict moral or ethical code, being unimpaired, and sound, whole and undivided, completeness.

"A real friend walks in when the rest of the world walks out."
Walter Winchell

In establishing yourself as a person of integrity, keep appointments and obligations. If you promise to do something, follow through. Commit fully when your word is on the line no matter how big or small the matter is. Be honest. Nothing damages one's character like being discovered as a liar. When you are asked a question, just tell the truth. Further, you can prove your trustworthiness by keeping secrets. Don't gossip about others. If you are asked for your opinion, be tactful yet truthful. Stand firm for your personal convictions. Let your behavior demonstrate your true character, what you really believe.

Stand up for your friends to prove that you are trustworthy. Do not acquire the reputation for being a "fair weather friend." Even if it means you will be inconvenienced in some way, always keep your word when you have obligated yourself to do something.

"Integrity is the essence of everything successful."
Richard Buckminster Fuller

To be trustworthy in all of life's situations is to have integrity. To have integrity is to hold to the kind of character and reputation that leads to personal success, happiness, and contentment. One who chooses to cultivate and maintain personal integrity in all of their relationships will ultimately have relationships that prove to be long-lasting and true. Making the effort to be a trustworthy person who displays integrity in all facets of life is a worthwhile endeavor.

"One of the truest tests of integrity is the blunt refusal to be compromised."
Chinua Achebe

Trustworthiness   Facilitator Guide

Introduction: Define trustworthiness.
              Why is trustworthiness important?
              Give an example of a person exemplifying trustworthiness.

Qualities that directly relate to a person being trustworthy (create a list)

- Honest- what is honesty
- Don't lie, cheat or steal
- Accountable
- Doing the right thing, making the right decisions

Are you a trustworthy person? Why or why not?

Group session questions:

- What does it mean to be honest?
- What does it mean to tell the truth?
- What qualities are important for a person to have within?
- Have you ever stolen anything?
- Have you ever lied?
- When is it alright to not tell the truth, steal, or cheat?
- Do you think you are a trustworthy person?

Write two paragraphs on the importance of you being a trustworthy person.

Peer Worksheet

Trustworthiness

Name: _____

Date: _____

Define Trustworthiness. _____

_____

Why is trust important? _____

_____

Give an example of a person that is trustworthy. _____

_____

List 5 things that are instilled in a trustworthy person:

    1. _____

    2. _____

    3. _____

    4. _____

    5. _____

Notes:

_____

_____

_____

What is the importance of being a trustworthy person?

_____

_____

_____

_____

_____

_____

_____

_____

_____

_____

_____

CARING

-is to be concerned, to look out for the welfare of others, to have an inclination, liking, affection

"Too often we underestimate the power of a touch, a smile, a kind
word, a listening ear, an honest compliment, or the smallest act of
caring, all of which have the potential to turn a life around."
Leo F. Buscaglia

A crucial element of building honorable character is that of developing a genuine interest in one's fellowman. Caring is not a trait that comes readily to some people. For many, it must be built over time. It is not inherent in an individual's makeup to exhibit concern for another. Other ways to demonstrate a caring attitude are to treat people with kindness, help people in need, be sensitive to other people's feelings, and never be mean, or deliberately hurtful. Think of how and what you do will affect others.

Ask yourself, "What does it mean to be a caring person?" Try to make a list of the do's and don'ts for being caring. List some specific examples of each type of behavior and compare the list with how you believe you measure up. If you determine that you are lacking in some areas, by all means try to make improvements. It is well worth the effort to develop genuine concern for others. Every time you interact with another person, ask yourself, "Will I behave in a caring way?" Make a decision to be an ethical, mature, caring person, no matter who you are dealing with. Although it may be easier to care for some people than for others, view the difficulties as a challenge. Make it your determination to show a caring attitude to them, as well.

"I feel the capacity to care is the thing which gives life its deepest significance."
Pablo Casals

Each person who desires to be a more caring individual should focus outside himself or herself and on the positive impact he or she can offer someone else. Begin with volunteering. Speak up when there is a need to perform an act of kindness! Reinforce your efforts to be caring by going out of your way to assist with chores at home and in other areas of life. Try to find things that you can do to make a difference in the life of someone else. Choose television programs that foster kindness, empathy, and compassion. Avoid programs that feature violence and anger. Observe others who you view as having a caring personality.

"The care of human life and happiness and not their destruction is
the first and only legitimate object of good government."
Thomas Jefferson

Caring   **Facilitator Guide**

Introduction: Define caring.
              Why is caring important?
              Give an example of a person that cares for himself.

Qualities that directly relate to a person caring for himself (create a list)

- Showing Feelings (sensitivity)
- Behaving mean or hurtful
- Being helpful when someone need something
- Generous
- Seeing if your behavior or actions affects others positively or negatively

Are you a person that cares for himself? Why or why not?

Group session questions:

- Why should a person care about himself?
- How can you tell if a person cares for himself?
- How do you practice caring for yourself?
- Name a person that cares for himself, how can you tell?
- How do people respect people that don't care about himself?

Write two paragraphs on the importance of caring about yourself.

Caring

Name: _____

Date: _____

Define caring. _____

_____

Why is caring about yourself important? _____

_____

Give an example of a person that cares for himself._____

_____

List 5 things that are instilled in a person that cares about himself:

    1. _____

    2. _____

    3. _____

    4. _____

    5. _____

Notes:

_____

_____

_____

What is the importance of a person care about himself?

_____

_____

_____

_____

_____

_____

_____

_____

_____

_____

_____

_____

DOING THE RIGHT THING

- involves being true to your own value system, even when it's not the popular thing to do, you may face ridicule, ostracism, even personal loss of one kind or another and yet you choose to do what is morally and ethically in your best interest and that of others

"A man cannot be comfortable without his own approval."
Mark Twain

One of the most difficult tasks in life to do is "the right thing." Doing what you think is right, not what your friends, family, teachers, boss, and society thinks is the right thing. By doing the right thing, you tend to get the same effort you give. Give value to people, help them and they will often want to reciprocate in like manner. Not everyone will respond in this way, but many will.

Doing what is right also raises one's own self-esteem. This is very important because when you do the right thing, you are sending signals to yourself. When you fail to do what is right, you don't feel good about yourself. You may experience emptiness or sadness, resulting in negative thoughts about yourself. Always strive to uphold what you believe to be fair and honest.

"What lies behind us and what lies before us are tiny matters compared to what lies within us."
Ralph Waldo Emerson

A powerful side effect of not doing the right thing is that sense you are less deserving. This can interfere with your future accomplishments in life. You might fail to think that you deserve success and might even rationalize that your failures are due to the fault of someone or something else, when in actuality, it is your own fault. Don't sabotage yourself. By doing the right thing, you can raise your self-esteem and feel like a person who deserves his/her success.

You might not be able to do the right thing in every situation. No one does. However you can make gradual improvements. Try to work toward a goal and look for opportunities to get better as time passes. Do not get caught up in striving for perfection. This will lead to negative feelings and self-doubt. Rather, make it your resolve to think before you act, carefully weigh the consequences of your decisions. Think of your actions and how they will affect others and may even have a long-term impact on your future success.

"Doing the right thing is more important than doing the thing right."
Peter F. Drucker

Doing the Right Thing   Facilitator Guide

Introduction: Define doing the right thing.
               Why is doing the right thing important?
               Give an example of a person that does the right thing.

Qualities that directly relate to a person doing the right thing (create a list)

- Fairness
- Consideration towards others
- Feelings for others
- Good hearted
- Good advice from trustworthy or respectful people
- Good results, not bad consequences

Are you a person that does the right thing all, most, some, or never the time? Why or why not?

Group session questions:

- Should a person be held responsible for doing what is right? Why or Why not?
- When you let someone down, how do you feel? How does the other person feel?
- What does it take to do the right thing?
- If you do the right thing, how does it make you feel inside?
- Does doing the right or wrong thing have any effect on others?
- If you don't do the right thing, what happens next?

Write a couple of paragraphs on the importance of you being a person that practices doing the right thing.

Doing the Right Thing

Name: _____

Date: _____

Define doing the right thing. _____

_____

Why is doing the right thing important? _____

_____

Give an example of a person that does the right thing. _____

_____

List 5 things that are instilled in a person that does the right thing:

    1. _____

    2. _____

    3. _____

    4. _____

    5. _____

Notes:

_____

_____

_____

What is the importance of being a person that does the right thing?

_____

_____

_____

_____

_____

_____

_____

_____

_____

_____

_____

BEING RESPONSIBLE

- being answerable, accountable, as for something within one's power, control, or management

"All business depends on men fulfilling their responsibilities."
Mahatma Gandhi

A responsible person assumes accountability for his or her actions, good or bad. It is good to own up to one's mistakes, even if it means there are undesirable consequences. By taking responsibility for your actions, both right and wrong, you are showing the world that you are a socially responsible person. Blaming others for your errors is an immature way to behave and one you should avoid.

Another consideration of being responsible is that we take care of ourselves and others. This requires being generous with our time and resources. Support the less fortunate through volunteering and other avenues of service to others. Take care of your own matters. If you need help, do not hesitate to ask someone you believe is capable of assisting you. When there is a need, step up and offer to do what you can to help.

"As human beings, we are endowed with freedom of choice, and
we cannot shuffle off our responsibility upon the shoulders of God
or nature. We must shoulder it ourselves. It is up to us."
Arnold Toynbee

Keeping promises is critical. If you commit to do something, follow through. Do what you say you will do, but know your limitations. Avoid making promises that you can't keep because this portrays you as unreliable. Be willing to complete tasks that you have been delegated. Understand that responsibility is earned; it is not something you're entitled to having. If someone is hesitant to give you responsibility, it may be because you have not demonstrated that you can be relied upon to do what is required. View yourself as capable of performing tasks assigned to you. Be trustworthy and motivated to take on potentially difficult projects. This builds the trust that others will have for you as a responsible individual.

" Every human being has a work to carry on within, duties to perform abroad, influence
to exert, which are peculiarly his, and which no conscience but his own can teach."
William Ellery Channing

Responsibility   Facilitator Guide

Introduction: Define responsibility.
                Why is responsibility important?
                Give an example of a person being responsible.

Qualities that directly relate to a person being responsible (create a list)

  • Dependable
  • Gets things done in a timely manner
  • Reliable
  • Doesn't blame others or make excuses

Are you a responsible person? Why or why not?

Group session questions:

  • Why should a person be responsible?
  • When you let someone down, how do you feel? How does the other person feel?
  • What is success? What does it take to be successful?
  • If you are responsible, how does it make you feel inside?
  • What does taking responsibility over a situation mean?
  • If a person fails, what happens next?

Write a couple of paragraphs on the importance of you being a responsible person.

Peer Worksheet

Responsibility

Name: _____

Date: _____

Define responsibility. _____
_____

Why is responsibility important? _____
_____

Example of a person that is responsible. _____
_____

List 5 things that are instilled in a responsible person:

     1. _____
     2. _____
     3. _____
     4. _____
     5. _____

Notes:

_____
_____
_____

What is the importance of being a responsible person?

_____
_____
_____
_____
_____
_____
_____
_____
_____
_____

LISTENING TO OTHERS

– giving attention with the ear; to incline one's intention closely for the purpose of hearing

"Let others confide in you. It may not help you, but it surely will help them."
Roger G. Imhoff

This trait is critically important in cultivating lasting and positive relationships. It displays respect for the opinions of others, whether we tend to agree or disagree with those opinions. It allows the speaker to communicate his or her own ideas and have them validated by the knowledge that we hear what they are attempting to say to us.

Listening is fundamentally important to having a meaningful dialogue with another. To listen is not merely to remain quiet while the other person is speaking. It involves giving your undivided focus to what is being said before giving a reply. One aspect of listening is that of putting yourself in the other person's "shoes" by showing empathy. When the other person is speaking, don't interrupt. Wait patiently until he or she has had ample opportunity to say what is on their mind. Follow and encourage the speaker with your body language. Communicate to him or her that you are giving them your full attention. Make an effort to ask meaningful questions. Practice the empathetic sounding back; give feedback when it is your turn to speak. It may be necessary for you to wait for the person to ask you for your opinion. Always try to reassure the speaker that all is well and that you genuinely care about his or her concerns.

"Listen, don't explain or justify."
William G. Dyer

If you make a whole-hearted effort to listen effectively, the speaker will believe that his or her conversation is being met with appreciation. Cultivating the art of effective listening will do much to strengthen the quality of your relationships with family, friends, future employers, and coworkers. Be the kind of person who is sought out for advice by showing that you are willing to listen. Be cautious to keep confidences. If someone shares a confidential matter or secret with you, have the integrity to keep the matter private. Never break a confidence. Doing so will mark you as one who will betray the privacy of another. Being a good listener is not only beneficial during your youth, but it is a quality that will prove beneficial for a lifetime.

"Learn to listen. Opportunity could be knocking very softly at your door."
Frank Tyger

Listening to Others   Facilitator Guide

Introduction: Define listening to others.
                   Why is listening to others important?
                   Give an example of a person that listens to others.

Qualities that directly relate to a person that listen to others (create a list)

- Doesn't talk while they are talking
- Makes eye contact
- Nods or gives appropriate body language feedback while they are talking
- Maybe repeat back to the person part of the conversation

Are you a good listener? Why or why not?

Group session questions:

- Why should a person be a good listener?
- When you don't listen to someone else, how do you feel? How does the other person feel?
- What does it take to be a good listener?
- If you are a good listener, how does it make you feel inside?
- How do your peers perceive you for being a good or bad listener?

Write two paragraphs on the importance of being a person that will listen to others well.

Peer Worksheet

Listening to Others

Name: _____

Date: _____

Define listening to others. _____
_____

Why is listening important? _____
_____

Give an example of a person that listens well. _____
_____

List 5 things that are instilled in a person that listen well:

    1. _____
    2. _____
    3. _____
    4. _____
    5. _____

Notes:

_____
_____
_____

What is the importance of being a good listener?

_____
_____
_____
_____
_____
_____
_____
_____
_____
_____
_____
_____

ASKING FOR HELP

- results in receiving what is necessary to accomplish a task or satisfy a need, it requires humility; acknowledging our dependence upon others for some of the resources we need

"There are no foolish questions and no man becomes a
fool until he has stopped asking questions."
Charles P. Steinmetz

There are so many tasks to be accomplished during the course of the day that it can become overwhelming. Seeking help from someone capable and willing to give it is often the solution, but asking for help can be difficult. Some people think asking for help may bruise their ego, while others are simply too shy or feel awkward about asking. Learn to take the pressure off yourself and ask for what is needed. It will save time, stress, and wasted effort.

"The art and science of asking is the source of all knowledge."
Thomas Berger

Know how to ask for help before frustration and anger takes over. This is the first and most important step in receiving help. Leave behind feelings of shame and embarrassment. Just because you're asking for help doesn't mean you are needy. You can save yourself time and stress if you enlist the help of someone in a position to help you. A good thing to remember is to state clearly what it is that would be helpful and be specific. People usually want to help if they know there is a need. Avoid whining if you feel you are doing too much. This turns people away. Be positive and you will have others willing to help you because of the kind of person you are.

Sometimes, you may feel intimidated about asking for help. If this is the case, talk to someone who you're close to – like a friend or family member. They might be able to point you in the right direction. Think about what will happen if the situation is not dealt with. Failing to get the help you need might result in matters becoming worse. Gather the courage, and humility, to ask for what you need. Then, always remember to say, "Thank you" when someone has been kind and considerate enough to come to your aid. Showing appreciation for help makes others willing to offer future assistance.

"Anything worth having is worth asking for. Some say yes and some say no."
Melba Colgrove

Asking for Help   Facilitator Guide

Introduction: Define asking for help.
                Why is knowing how to ask for help important?
                Give an example of a person asks for help.

Qualities that directly relate to a person that will ask for help (create a list)

- Do not be shameful/prideful
- Will you be able to finish the task
- Knowing if the person is the right person to ask
- Do you need help to complete the task
- After someone helps you, what is the proper way to thank them (different situations, warrant different thank you responses)

Are you a person that asks for help when you need it? Why or why not?

Group session questions:

- When you need help, do you ask?
- How can you tell if you need help?
- How should you ask people for help?
- Name a person that knows how to ask people for help?
- How do people respect people that know how to ask for help and are thankful?

Write two paragraphs on the importance of asking for help and being thankful.

Asking for Help

Name: _____

Date: _____

Define asking for help. _____
_____

Why should a person know how to ask for help? _____
_____

Give an example of a person that knows how to ask for help. _____
_____

List 5 things that are instilled in a person that knows how to ask for help:

    1. _____
    2. _____
    3. _____
    4. _____
    5. _____

Notes:

_____
_____
_____

What is the importance of a person that knows how to ask for help?

_____
_____
_____
_____
_____
_____
_____
_____
_____
_____
_____

DEALING WITH FEELINGS

– an emotion or emotional perception or attitude that portrays sympathy or fellow feeling

"Compassion will cure more sins than condemnation"
Henry Ward Beecher

In confronting one's own feelings, it is helpful to acknowledge that you are happy, angry, sad, fearful, embarrassed, or whatever you are feeling at the moment. If necessary, you may want to relax and take time to sort through conflicting emotions. Think about ways to help yourself and then take decisive action to improve your situation. Realize that no one always feels happy; there are good days and bad days. Emotions tend to fluctuate from day-to-day, depending on the circumstances. Pay attention to what triggers your negative feelings and look for ways to avoid the issues that bring about bad experiences. Treat yourself kindly. Do not berate yourself for mistakes or poor decisions because this makes you feel worse. Do something nice for yourself, such as a walk with a trusted friend; watch a movie, or just a break from your normal routine. Give yourself time to feel better. Seek out a trusted adult in whom you can confide your feelings. Usually, whenever we give a voice to our negative feelings, they are minimized and do not appear so overwhelming after all.

"Compassion is the basis of all morality."
Arthur Schopenhaur

In showing compassion for others, it is necessary to step into the other person's shoes – to make an effort to consider what the other person is feeling. This is not easy if you have never attempted to show sincere compassion. Think about how you would react if you were in the same situation as the one for whom you wish to show compassion. Try to display a genuine concern for the other person's problem or predicament. Show that you care by presenting possible solutions to their dilemma. If possible, help the person find outside resources that may help alleviate their concerns. Speak calmly, rationally, and with respect for the other person's feelings. If they are feeling helpless about their problems, try to reassure them that the concerns usually work out in time. Try to engage the person in some type of positive activity that will take his mind off the immediate distress he may be going through.

"Compassion is not weakness and concern for the unfortunate is not socialism."
Hubert H. Humphrey

Dealing with Feeling   Facilitator Guide

Introduction: Define feelings?
               Why is learning how to deal with feelings important?
               Give an example of a person that shows their feelings- is that good or bad?

Characteristics that directly relate to a person that deals with their feelings (create a list)

- How do you handle your emotions
- Do you judge things in a right and wrong manner
- Considerations for others feeling
- Are you spoiled and want everything you see
- Do you get things you want

Are you a person that every experienced being hurt or happily surprised? How? How did you respond to the situation?

Group session questions:

- Why should every person learn about their feelings and what they mean?
- How can you tell if a person is happy or sad?
- How do you practice dealing with the great things and bad things?
- Name a person that has been disappointed and bounced back?
- What does it take to bounce back from being from a bad situation?

Write two paragraphs on the importance of learning how to deal with feelings.

Peer Worksheet

Dealing with Feelings

Name: _____

Date: _____

Define Feelings. _____

_____

Why is dealing with your feelings important?_____

_____

Give an example of a person that shows their feelings, whether they are good or bad._____

_____

List 5 things that can help a person deal with their feelings:

    1. _____

    2. _____

    3. _____

    4. _____

    5. _____

Notes:

_____

_____

_____

What is the importance of a person learning how to deal with their feelings?

_____

_____

_____

_____

_____

_____

_____

_____

_____

_____

_____

DEALING WITH DISAPPOINTMENT

– let down, dissatisfaction over some life event or circumstance

"We must accept finite disappointment, but never lose infinite hope."
Dr. Martin Luther King, Jr.

Everyone makes plans, has dreams, and sets goals. Not all dreams, goals or plans work out the way we hope for. Our attempts may end in victory or defeat, and when met with failure, we sometimes face severe feelings of disappointment. Because it is important to learn to deal with disappointment, Dr. Martin Luther King, Jr. suggested that one way of coping is to accept the defeat or letdown. Disappoint can lead to anguish and stressful times in a person's life. Some useful tips for coping with feelings of disappointment include: venting your feelings; reflecting on experiences that were disappointing and how you managed to deal with them; and deciding that let downs occur from time-to-time, and they are soon forgotten.

"Disappointment is a sort of bankruptcy; the bankruptcy of a
soul that expends too much in hope and expectation."
Eric Hoffer

Dealing with disappointment is a fact of life. How you deal with these small defeats will determine whether you become a confident person, who is in control of your life, or simply a victim. If you become angry because of a disappointment, try to assess the reason for your feelings. Realize that there is no reason for self-blame. Sometimes, circumstances just don't meet our expectations. This kind of reaction will only make the situation worse. You might begin to feel sorry for yourself, which only leads to further disappointment. Step back and try to view the situation from a different perspective. Acknowledge that disappointments often strengthen your character and make you a more resilient person that can face adversities when necessary.

"The sudden disappointment of a hope leaves a scar which the
ultimate fulfillment of that hope never entirely removes."
Thomas Hardy

Learning to use disappointments to your advantage is just one way to grow in your abilities and maturity. You can have a better outlook if you master the ability to cope with, and enhance your development by successfully meet the challenges of disappointments.

"Suspense is worse than disappointment."
Robert Burns

Dealing with Disappointment   Facilitator Guide

Introduction: Define disappointment?
Why is it important to know how to deal with disappointment?
Give an example of a person you have seen being disappointed.

Characteristics that directly relate to a person being disappointed (create a list)

- Experiencing failure
- Doesn't receive what they want
- Has low self-esteem
- Anger towards a situation
- Upset with others

Are you a person that every experienced being disappointed? How did you respond to the situation?

Group session questions:

- Why should every person learn about disappointment?
- How can you tell if a person is disappointed?
- How do you practice dealing with the disappointment?
- Name a person that has been disappointed and bounced back?
- What does it take to bounce back from being disappointed?

Write two paragraphs on the importance of learning how to deal with disappointment.

Dealing with Disappointment

Name: _____

Date: _____

Define disappointment. _____

_____

Why is dealing with disappointment important? _____

_____

Example of a person that has been disappointed. _____

_____

List 5 things that can help a person deal with disappointment:

    1. _____

    2. _____

    3. _____

    4. _____

    5. _____

Notes:

_____

_____

_____

What is the importance of a person learning how to deal with disappointment?

_____

_____

_____

_____

_____

_____

_____

_____

_____

_____

FAIRNESS

– to be just and equal in treatment of everyone; to be impartial and non-discriminatory

"It is not fair to ask of others what you are unwilling to do yourself."
Eleanor Roosevelt

A fair person is one who makes decisions without playing favorites. He or she does not take advantage of others, or unjustly places blame on others. If your desire is to become a fair-minded person, learn to take turns and share with others. Play by the rules, and demonstrate good sportsmanship. Allow competition to guide you to do your best, not get the best of your opponents. Keeping an open mind and practicing patience in hearing what the other person has to say are important. Listen attentively to the opinions of others, whether you agree with them or not. In a disagreement, try to see the other person's side of the matter.

"Do more than belong: participate. Do more than care: help. Do more than believe: practice. Do more than be fair: be kind. Do more than forgive: forget. Do more than dream: work."
William Arthur Ward

It is also good to realize that almost every decision you make (even small ones) affects other people. Therefore, it is important to try to maintain an objective attitude when sizing up a situation. Treat people the way you want to be treated. Avoid being critical or negative. Look for something positive to say to improve an otherwise tense situation. When it is necessary for you to decide the outcome of a matter, be prepared to give your reason for the decision that you make. Listen carefully to both sides before jumping to a conclusion. Respect the speaker as he or she states his or her viewpoints. This will help reinforce in others that you are at least attempting to be impartial. No one wants to be judged harshly, even if they are in the wrong. Show courtesy to everyone involved. At home, if you are asked to perform certain tasks that your siblings are not asked to perform, do not whine and complain. Rather, ask your parents if you may have the opportunity to express how you feel. More is gained when you respectfully request a hearing ear than if one is demanded.

Try to assess matters objectively. Never conclude that you have all the answers. A wise person learns to become fair, it does not happen automatically.

"Fairness is what justice really is."
Potter Stewart

Dealing with Fairness

Facilitator Guide

Introduction: Define fairness.
Why is being fair important?
Give an example of a person that treats people fairly.

Qualities that directly relate to a person that treats people fair (create a list)

- Be open minded
- Try putting yourself in the other person's shoes
- Be considerate of all the people involved
- Do not take advantage of other people
- If there are rules or laws, follow them
- Doesn't lie to get ahead

Are you a person that is fair? Why or why not?

Group session questions:

- Why should a person be fair?
- How can you tell if a person is fair?
- How do you practice being a fair person?
- Name a person that is fair, how can you tell?
- How do people respect people that are fair?

Write two paragraphs on the importance of being fair.

Peer Worksheet

Dealing with Fairness

Name: _____

Date: _____

Define fairness. _____

_____

Why is being fair important? _____

_____

Give an example of a person that is fair. _____

_____

List 5 things that are instilled in a person that is fair:

1. _____
2. _____
3. _____
4. _____
5. _____

Notes:

_____

_____

_____

What is the importance of a person being fair?

_____

_____

_____

_____

_____

_____

_____

_____

_____

_____

_____

BULLYING

- is the characteristic of being overbearing, habitually badgering and imposing one's will on others by either physical force or intimidation

"Courage is fire, and bullying is smoke."
Benjamin Disraeli

Two of the main reasons that people are bullied are due to their appearance and/or their social status. Bullies pick on people they don't think fit in, maybe because of how they look, act, think, or where they live. It could also be due to their race, religion, or because their bullies have low self-esteem issues and feel better when they are picking on someone else.

Some bullies attack their targets physically, which can mean anything from shoving, tripping, punching, hitting, or even sexual assault. Still others use a form of psychological control or verbal insults to establish themselves as in charge. Bullying may involve exclusion as in refusing to include others in group settings such as; in the school cafeteria, on sports teams, or in group projects at school. The bully may taunt or tease the victim or send threatening messages via text messaging or e-mail or post cruel remarks on a website. This is known as cyber bullying. Whatever the format for bullying, it is an unacceptable practice that should never be tolerated.

If you find that you have become the target of a bully or bullies, immediately take steps in protecting yourself. This does not mean that you retaliate. Seek the help of an authority figure such as; a teacher, principal, parent, or other adult who can intervene on your behalf. Do not be intimidated into keeping silent. It is important to expose the situation so that you can receive the help you need.

Bullying is a very big problem in today's society. It is a cowardly, hateful practice and should be avoided by people who seek to advance their status in life. Mature people do not engage in bullying. They realize that this is a serious character flaw that does lasting damage to those upon whom it is inflicted. Often bullies grow up to commit acts of bullying on others and the cycle is then perpetuated. Not only is this offensive behavior, it can result in highly undesirable consequences, including incarceration. Anyone who has noticed tendencies toward bullying would be wise to curtail such inclinations before him or her become ingrained.

"True courage is cool and calm. The bravest of men have the least of a brutal, bullying insolence, and in the very time of danger are found the most serene and free."
Lord Shaftesbury

Bullying   Facilitator Guide

Introduction: Define bullying.
                       Why is it important not to be a bully?
                       Give an example of a person that is a bully.

Qualities that directly relate to a person that is a bully (create a list)

- Bullies try to intimidate smaller weaker people
- Bullies try to take advantage of less unfortunate people
- Bullies try to threaten people if you don't get what you want
- Bullies get angry when you don't get their way and still try to push the issue

Are you a person that bullies other people? Why or why not?

Group session questions:

- Why should a person not be a bully?
- How can you tell if a person is a bully?
- How do you practice not being a bully?
- Name a person that's not a bully, how can you tell?
- How do people respect people that are not bullies?

Write two paragraphs on the importance of not being a bully.

Peer Worksheet

Bullying

Name: _____

Date: _____

Define Bullying. _____

_____

Why is it important not to be a bully? _____

_____

Give an example of a person that is a bully. _____

_____

List 5 things that are characteristics of a person that is a bully:

    1. _____

    2. _____

    3. _____

    4. _____

    5. _____

Notes:

_____

_____

_____

What is the importance of a person, to not be a bully?

_____

_____

_____

_____

_____

_____

_____

_____

_____

_____

_____

PREJUDICE

– an unfavorable opinion or feeling formed beforehand or without knowledge,
a preconceived judgment or action of another in disregard of one's rights

"Never be bullied into silence. Never allow yourself to be made a victim.
Accept no one's definition of your life, but define yourself."
Harvey S. Firestone

A prejudiced person is one who makes assumptions about someone or something before having adequate knowledge to do so with guaranteed accuracy. The word prejudice, itself, is commonly used to refer to an unfair judgment toward people based on race, social class, gender, ethnicity, age, disability, political beliefs, religion, sexual orientation, or other personal characteristics. It also means beliefs without knowledge of the facts and may include any unreasonable attitude that is unusually resistant to rational influence. Prejudice afflicts many people and it has been said that everyone, to some degree or extent, has some type of prejudices whether inherent, or cultivated from personal experiences.

Racism is a form of prejudice, and may include different types of discrimination. By prejudging a member of a race, or of an ethnic group, a racist decides how that person will act or speak and what sort of capabilities and potential he or she has. Even before getting to know the person, the racist then chooses to treat that person differently from others. Prejudice is a serious character flaw and is to be avoided at all costs. It is inexcusable and although common, is not to be viewed as acceptable in any of its forms.

To avoid becoming a prejudiced person you should get to know a person on an individual basis before you decide whether you like him or her or not. Realize that you will not like everyone, but you do need to respect them as an individual and spend time with them before you make a judgment. Acknowledge that your way is not the only way. Observe the Golden Rule: "Treat others as you would have them treat you." Think about how you would feel if you were treated the way you behave toward others. Try to look at your motives and actions from a different perspective. Make an effort to learn about different cultures and people to understand differences between yourself and others. Education allows you to separate truth from fiction when it comes to how you perceive other people. After learning about differences, respect those differences. Even if you don't agree with someone, you can respect their opinion. This will help to cultivate within you an avoidance of prejudicial tendencies.

"Preconceived notions are the locks on the door to wisdom."
Merry Browne

Prejudice   Facilitator Guide

Introduction: Define Prejudice.
              Why is important not to be prejudice?
              Give an example of a person that is prejudice.

Characteristics that directly relate to a person that is prejudice (create a list)

- Don't pre-judge people
- Does prejudice just have to be with people? What about material things?
- How do you treat other people? Why?
- What do you know about things outside your community and culture?

Are you a prejudice person? Why or why not?

Group session questions:
- Why should a person not be prejudice?
- How can you tell if a person is prejudice or not?
- How do you practice not being prejudice?
- Name a person that is prejudice. How can you tell?
- How do people respect people that are prejudice?

Write two paragraphs on the importance of not being prejudice.

Peer Worksheet

Prejudice

Name: _____
Date: _____

Define Prejudice. _____
_____

Why is important not to be prejudice? _____
_____

Give an example of a person that is prejudice. _____
_____

List 5 things that are instilled in a person that is prejudice:

1. _____
2. _____
3. _____
4. _____
5. _____

Notes:

_____
_____
_____

What is the importance of being a person that is not prejudice?

_____
_____
_____
_____
_____
_____
_____
_____
_____
_____
_____

BEING FRIENDS

– someone attached to another by feelings of affection or personal regard

"Hold a true friend with both hands."
Nigerian Proverb

Being a good friend is the goal that most people aspire. It requires many characteristics that need to be developed over time. A person doesn't automatically become a "friend" in the true sense of the word just by becoming acquainted with someone. Friendships are born from getting to know a person's likes, dislikes, habits, value system, and personality. Generally, people bond as friends when they have common interests and ideologies. In some cases the opposite is true. People may be drawn to other people that are polar opposites of themselves because of the differences in personalities but typically friends share similar traits.

"A friend is a gift you give yourself."
Robert Louis Stevenson

Good friends are good listeners. They try to understand each other's point of view. In trying to be a good friend, it is always helpful to show respect, even when there is a difference of opinion. A true friend is reliable and trustworthy. He or she can be depended upon to give support and empathy when problems arise. They realize that it is important to respect each other's personal space and to avoid asking invasive questions about private matters, unless such a conversation is initiated by the other person. It's appropriate to be there with a "shoulder to cry on," but at the same time, do not cross boundaries that could be considered "meddling." Being someone's friend does not give you liberty to interfere without first being asked for your opinion or input. Respect is a must in forming and maintaining lasting friendships.

"You can make more friends in two months by becoming interested in other people than you can in two years by trying to get other people interested in you."
Dale Carnegie

A real friend is not one who will betray your trust. He or she can be entrusted with a confidential matter or "secret" without fear of disclosing the information to others. Being a "blabbermouth" is not a desirable trait of a friend. Telling another's business will make it known that you are not trustworthy and when your other friends learn of this, no one will want to confide in you. In other words, your reputation will suffer damage that could last a long time.

"Silence is a true friend that never betrays."
Confucius

Being Friends   Facilitator Guide

Introduction: Define being a friend.
               Why is it important to be a friend?
               Give an example of a person that is a friend.

Qualities that directly relate to a person that is a friend (create a list)

- Dependable
- Trustworthy
- Good listener
- Cares about you
- Helps you in times of need

Are you a person that is a good friend? Why or why not?

Group session questions:

- Why should a person be a good friend?
- How can you tell if a person is a friend?
- How do you practice being a friend?
- Name a person that is a friend. How can you tell?
- How do people respect people that are good friends?

Write two paragraphs on the importance of being a good friend.

Peer Worksheet

Being Friends

Name: _____

Date: _____

Define being a friend._____

_____

Why is being a good friend important?_____

_____

Give an example of a person that is a good friend. _____

_____

List 5 things that are instilled in a person that is a good friend:

    1. _____

    2. _____

    3. _____

    4. _____

    5. _____

Notes:

_____

_____

_____

What is the importance of a person being a good friend?

_____

_____

_____

_____

_____

_____

_____

_____

_____

_____

_____

_____

COOPERATION

– an act or instance of working or acting together for a common purpose or benefit

"It is through cooperation, rather than conflict, that your greatest successes will be delivered."
Ralph Charell

Cooperation comes from a motive within our self to work with, rather than against; a person, effort, or movement. It requires a desire to be a part of the team and to show respect for the contribution of others. To achieve something as part of a team, we need to be willing to communicate effectively. Listen carefully to what others are saying and try to understand what their expectations are. Be open to compromise when there is a serious conflict. Do your part to contribute to the group effort, and show appreciation for what is done by others.

"We are all dependent on one another, every soul of us on earth."
George Bernard Shaw

Being a cooperative person conveys the idea of doing your share, being polite, and balancing giving input with seeking input in interactions with others. This is necessary to understand their actions and reactions. It is best to offer suggestions when asked for input, other than that, wait until your advice is solicited. Cooperation involves showing a sincere interest in the preferences of others. Do not insist on having it your way at all times. Acknowledge that the other person's ideas and concepts are just as valid as your own.

Cooperation is the result of social division of labor. One person is limited in what he or she can accomplish. Therefore, the need arises to include the efforts of others to attain a specific goal. Teamwork is a large part of developing a cooperative spirit. Learning dependency upon friends, family members, coworkers and other members of society is inevitable. Often, it becomes obvious that others need our assistance, as well. When called upon to do something for someone else, we should readily step forward and do the best we can to render whatever aid is needed. When we do so willingly, it becomes easier to make this a part of who we are. To meet the requirements of success, developing a cooperative attitude is vital. Realize that no one is completely independent, and as such, we will have the opportunity to display that we are a part of the team. Each member of society has the privilege and the obligation to do their part to work together.

"We may have all come on different ships, but we're in the same boat now."
Martin Luther King, Jr.

Cooperation   Facilitator Guide

Introduction: Define cooperation.
                Why is cooperation important?
                Give an example of a person that knows how to cooperate.

Qualities that directly relate to a person cooperates (create a list)

- Shares
- Compromise
- Takes turns
- Makes people feel like they are apart of the project
- Doesn't leave anyone out

Are you a person that knows how to cooperate? Why or why not?

Group session questions:

- Why should a person cooperate?
- How can you tell if a person knows how to cooperate?
- How do you practice cooperating?
- Name a person that cooperates, how can you tell?
- How do people respect people that know how to cooperate?

Write two paragraphs on the importance of cooperation.

Cooperation

Name: _____

Date: _____

Define cooperation. _____

_____

Why is cooperation important? _____

_____

Give an example of a person that knows how to cooperate. _____

_____

List 5 things that are instilled in a person that cooperate:

    1. _____

    2. _____

    3. _____

    4. _____

    5. _____

Notes:

_____

_____

_____

What is the importance of a person being able to cooperate?

_____

_____

_____

_____

_____

_____

_____

_____

_____

_____

_____

CONTROLLING ANGER

– a strong feeling of displeasure and belligerence aroused by a wrong; wrath, ire

"For every minute that you are angry, you lose sixty seconds of happiness."
Ralph Waldo Emerson

Anger can be very destructive to yourself and others. Not only can it harm you on the outside, but internally as well. It is a feeling, or destructive emotion which can take over without warning. A strong resentment to being treated unjustly will provoke anger quickly. However, there is such a thing as legitimate anger. This is a reaction to being cheated, lied to, having something stolen from you, or having been violated in some other way. This justified anger may be amplified by frustration, where one cannot do anything to rectify the situation, either because it is in the past and done, or because the cause cannot or will not be changed. Dwelling on this type of anger often causes extreme emotional damage.

"Speak when you are angry and you'll make the best speech you'll ever regret."
Dr. Lawrence J. Peter

Learn to identify your anger. Determine whether it arises from a legitimate cause, or from expectation. When it is from a legitimate cause, such as being robbed or burglarized, the resulting bitterness is compounded when there is no justice to remedy your situation. One allows the perpetrator to control one's feelings endlessly, not only in the past, but also in the future. It is this type of anger that must be dealt with, in order to; prevent lasting harm to your emotional health. Understand that unresolved anger is often directed unfairly at others by stereotype, as individual persons, groups, or organizations. Being unable or unwilling to confront the source of one's anger can cause a person to create a general category resembling a certain character of the source and attack those of that type to get justice. It is unfair and unethical to treat innocent people in this manner.

"Anger is never without a reason, but seldom with a good one."
Benjamin Franklin

Before indulging in anger, try to be realistic. Do not expect others to share the same standards, values, and expectations as oneself. Perhaps the most common expectation is expecting others to conform to one's own standards. Don't assume that others are intentionally trying to make you angry.

"Anger dwells only in the bosom of fools."
Albert Einstein

Controlling Anger   Facilitator Guide

Introduction: Define anger.
                    Why is it important to be able to control your anger?
                    Give an example of a person that knows how to control their anger.

Qualities that directly relate to a person appreciating themselves (create a list)

- Try being calm
- Think of consequences
- Understanding what the problem is
- Put yourself in winnable situations

Are you a person that can control their anger? Why or why not?

Group session questions:

- Why should a person be able to control their anger?
- How can you tell if a person can control their anger?
- How do you practice controlling your anger? What techniques can you use?
- Name a person that can control their anger. How can you tell?
- How do people respect people that know how to control their anger?

Write two paragraphs on the importance of being able to control their anger.

Peer Worksheet

Controlling Anger

Name: _____

Date: _____

Define anger. _____

_____

Why is being able to control anger important? _____

_____

Give an example of a person that controls their anger. _____

_____

List 5 things that are instilled in a person that can control their anger:

    1. _____

    2. _____

    3. _____

    4. _____

    5. _____

Notes:

_____

_____

_____

What is the importance of a person being able to control their anger?

_____

_____

_____

_____

_____

_____

_____

_____

_____

_____

_____

SAYING "NO"

– an answer given to indicate an unwillingness or refusal to comply with a certain request

"Stay committed to your decisions, but stay flexible in your approach."
Tom Robbins

Saying "no" is not always easy, especially for some people. However, in life it is often necessary to refuse a request. You should know how to do so effectively, yet with respect for the person who is making the request. First, realize that if you say "yes" too often, you will likely become the victim of those who would take advantage of you. Saying "no" is an acquired skill that helps an individual to have focus and direction in life. Others may pressure you to say "yes" but before you do, consider all the ramifications of what your commitment to their request involves. When you do say "no" you can expect the person who hears it to react negatively, sometimes mildly, sometimes strongly. Be prepared to stand your ground and offer your reason for saying "no" if you feel the need to do so.

Many people were raised to be "people pleasers." The word "no" dropped out of their vocabulary at an early age. As a result, they eventually find that some may perceive them as "doormats," and assume that they are willing to comply with whatever is asked of them. Instead of adopting this behavior, try to strike a reasonable balance between agreeing and disagreeing with the wishes of other people. Your argument for saying either "yes" or "no" should be valid, not whimsical. When someone makes a request, remember that it is perfectly acceptable to ask for time to think about it. It is not always necessary to make a decision on the spot. After giving careful thought to whether this is something you want to do, be committed to stand firm with your decision. If you appear to be indecisive, the person making the request will likely view this as an opportunity to change your mind. Stick with what you believe to be in your own best interest, and the best interest of others, as well.

"Have the courage to say no. Have the courage to face the truth. Do the right thing because it is right. These are the magic keys to living your life with integrity."
W. Clement Stone

Saying No   Facilitator Guide

Introduction: Define saying "No."
                Why is it important to be able to say "No?"
                Give an example of a person that can say "No."

Qualities that directly relate to a person that says "No" (create a list)

- Believes in him or herself
- Leadership skills
- Confident person
- Knows how to solve problems
- Considers other people feelings

Are you a person that says "No"? Why or why not?

Group session questions:

- Why should a person feel comfortable saying "No?"
- How can you tell if a person is comfortable saying "No?"
- How do you practice saying "No?"
- Name a person that says "No," how can you tell?
- How does a person respect people that say "No?"

Write two paragraphs on the importance of saying "No"

Peer Worksheet

Saying "No"

Name: _____

Date: _____

Define saying "No." _____

_____

Why is it important to be able to Say "No?" _____

_____

Give an example of a person that says "No." _____

_____

List 5 things that are instilled in a person that comfortable saying "No":

    1. _____

    2. _____

    3. _____

    4. _____

    5. _____

Notes:

_____

_____

_____

What is the importance of a person being able to say "No?"

_____

_____

_____

_____

_____

_____

_____

_____

_____

_____

_____

_____

RESOLVING CONFLICT

– to come into collision or disagreement; be contradictory, in opposition

"The greatest challenge to any thinker is stating the
problem in a way that will allow a solution."
Bertrand Russell

The fact conflict exists is a definite reason to develop skills to address issues that arise between individuals with differing opinions, ideologies, personalities, and attitudes. A very important step to take is to stop: don't allow the conflict to worsen. Clearly state what the conflicts are and think of positive options to resolve them. Choose a positive option rather than a negative one and be sure to include the feelings of the other person. Make your choice based upon what is agreeable with both of you. Agree to resolve the conflict. Making a concerted effort to reach a mutual understanding and outcome will help facilitate the resolution.

When approaching any disagreement, increased understanding is required. The discussion needed to resolve conflict expands people's awareness of the situation, giving them an insight into how they can achieve their own goals without undermining those of others. However, if conflict is not handled effectively, the results can be damaging. There is a risk of cultivating a strong dislike for the other person and teamwork is hindered. Be patient. Take turns talking and refrain from interrupting when the other person is speaking. Be clear and specific about the problem. Remember to be an attentive listener. Use your brains, not your hands and strive for a compromise that will be agreeable to both parties. Listen with empathy, which entails putting yourself in the other person's place. Try to view matters from his or her perspective, not just your own.

"People who fight fire with fire usually wind up with ashes."
Abigail Van Buren

In resolving conflict, look for motives, sometimes different people will see the same situation in a different light. Be open to a solution that you might not necessarily come up with yourself. Do not insist on having everything go your way. Be flexible and open to suggestions from an objective third party who may be in a position to offer a clear understanding of what needs to be done. Pursue ways to resolve the conflict and continue to improve your skills in this area.

"Always pass a plate of forgiveness before each verbal feast."
Anabel Jensen

Resolving Conflict   Facilitator Guide

Introduction: Define conflict.
              Why is resolving conflict important?
              Give an example of a person that resolves conflict.

Qualities that directly relate to a person can resolve conflict (create a list)

- Being humble in confrontational situations
- Learning how to solve problems
- Positive minded people
- People that can think of other options

Are you a person that can resolve conflict? Why or why not?

Group session questions:

- Why should a person be able to resolve conflict?
- How can you tell if a person can resolve a conflict?
- How do you practice resolving conflict and staying out of conflicts?
- Name a person that knows how to resolve conflict. How can you tell?
- Why people respect people that can stay out of confrontations?

Write two paragraphs on the importance of being able to resolve conflicts.

Peer Worksheet

Resolving Conflicts

Name: _____

Date: _____

Define conflicts. _____

_____

Why is resolving conflicts important?_____

_____

Give an example of a person that knows how to resolve conflicts._____

_____

List 5 things that are instilled in a person that can resolve conflicts:

    1. _____

    2. _____

    3. _____

    4. _____

    5. _____

Notes:

_____

_____

_____

What is the importance of a person being able to resolve conflicts?

_____

_____

_____

_____

_____

_____

_____

_____

_____

_____

_____

_____

ACHIEVEMENT

- acquiring something positive for oneself or gaining something
positive for someone else or a company

"Winners compare their achievements with their goals, while losers
compare their achievements with those of other people."
Nido Qubein

Accomplishing or achieving something means to bring success, to carry through, to gain, or to bring about an intended result. There are several helpful suggestions regarding how to achieve or accomplish a desired goal. To start, a deep desire for the goal or resolution is needed. Visualize yourself achieving the goal. Make a definite plan; be specific about how you intend to make your desire a reality. Commit to achieving what you've set out to do. Do not be discouraged by the negative opinions of others. Included in your specific plan of action should be a designated time slot in which you will work toward the particular components of your goals. Be consistent in keeping the appointments you make with others and yourself. Try not to be distracted from sitting down at the scheduled time to work on your tasks.

"That some achieve great success is proof to all that others can achieve it as well."
Abraham Lincoln

Organization is critical to success. Nothing positive can be accomplished in chaos. If your workspace is not tidy and organized, it makes it more difficult to put into action your ideas. Enlist the aid of others in your goals. Find people, resources, agencies, and whatever help is available to make your plans come to life. Review your progress regularly. Do not become complacent about seeking information. Make a timeline for accomplishing the minor goals that contribute to realizing the major goals.

As you manage to achieve these goals in small increments, reward yourself! Acknowledge what you have already accomplished before you proceed to do even more. This will give your morale a boost and instill confidence in your ability to achieve the desired outcome. Be willing to suffer setbacks as they are all a part of the process. Don't feel defeated or cheated out of your dream. Learn from your mistakes and know what not to do in the future. Never become impatient and feel as if you are not making progress. The fact your ideas are still important to you means that you can move forward and accomplish the goals you have set for yourself.

"You have to learn the rules of the game and then you have to play better than anyone else."
Albert Einstein

Achievement   Facilitator Guide

Introduction: Define achievement.
               Why is achievement important?
               Give an example of a person that is an achiever.

Qualities that directly relate to a person achievements (create a list)

- Can see the invisible to achieve the impossible
- Reaches for the stars
- Has a plan and see's the plan through
- Desires to finish
- Has obtainable goals
- Successful

Are you a person that achieves? Why or why not?

Group session questions:

- Why should a person set small goals to achieve things?
- How can you tell if a person is achieving some of their goals?
- How do you practice achieving success?
- Name a person that is successful?
- How do people respect people that achieve their goals?

Write two paragraphs on the importance of achieving goals and being successful.

Peer Worksheet

Achievement

Name: _____

Date: _____

Define achievement. _____

_____

Why is achievement important? _____

_____

Give an example of a person that is successful. _____

_____

List 5 things that are instilled in a person that achieve goals and are successful:

    1. _____
    2. _____
    3. _____
    4. _____
    5. _____

Notes:

_____

_____

_____

What is the importance of a person achieving goals and being successful?

_____

_____

_____

_____

_____

_____

_____

_____

_____

_____

_____

_____

About the Author

Jarmel Bell graduated from Marked Tree High School in 1997. He went to the University of Arkansas to play football. He was a walk-on (a player without a scholarship). He only played 4 weeks before quitting. Many people wondered why he quit, but the lack of having a mentor to help him during this transition left him without guidance. Jarmel didn't understand you have to crawl before you walk. He didn't understand the concept of having to pay your dues.

Jarmel left the University of Arkansas and spent 4 years in the United States Air force, earning a honorable discharge. He attended Arkansas State University earning his Bachelor in Mid-Level Education and his Masters in Science Education with an emphasis in Theory and Practice. During his college days, he worked at Families Incorporation as a mentor; he worked at Consolidated Youth Services (Juvenile detention Center) as a Youth Counselor. He has been a school teacher for 5 years. He taught 7th & 8th grade math for 2 years, and has been a math coach for 3 years.

Jarmel does consultant work, professional development, speaking engagements, leadership training, and has a great character education program for students, both male and female. If you would like more information about these programs, visit www.thequote-online.com